UNTiL the COWS COME HOMe

and Other Expressions about ANIMALS

SANDY DONOVAN

Illustrated by
AARON BLECHA

Ŀ Lerner Publications Company
MINNEAPOLIS

Lerner Publications Company
A division of Lerner Publishing Group, Inc.
241 First Avenue North
Minneapolis, MN 55401 U.S.A.

Website address: www.lernerbooks.com

Library of Congress Cataloging-in-Publication Data

Donovan, Sandra, 1967–
    Until the cows come home : and other
expressions about animals / by Sandy Donovan.
        p.   cm. — (It's just an expression)
    Includes index.
    ISBN 978-0-7613-7890-7 (lib. bdg. : alk. paper)
    1. English language—Idioms—Juvenile literature.
2. Figures of speech—Juvenile literature. 3. Animals—
Juvenile literature. I. Title.
PE1460.D68 2013
428.1—dc23   2011035429

Manufactured in the United States of America
1 – PC – 7/15/12

TABLE of CONTENTS

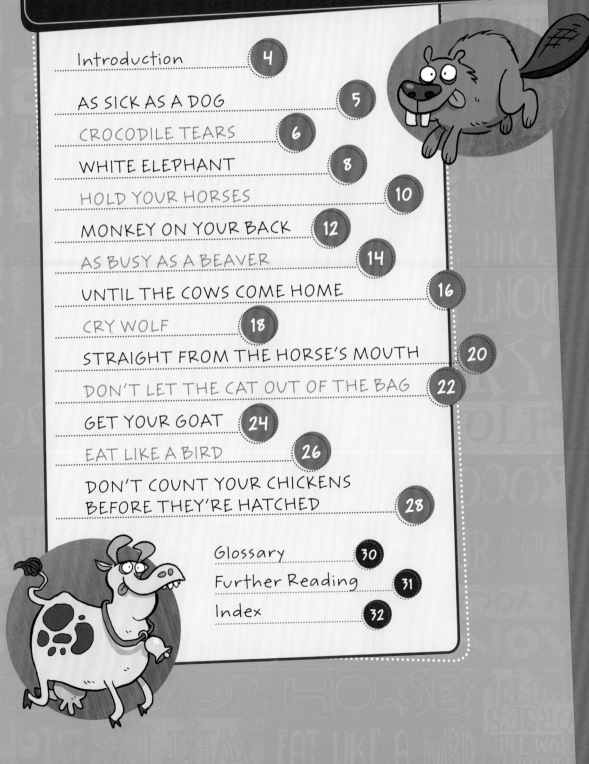

INTRODUCTION

Aiden doesn't know what to do. He's got a **monkey on his back,** and he's been as **busy as a beaver,** studying **till the cows come home.** But he's still panicked about the big math test tomorrow. He's trying not to let it **get his goat,** but he's so stressed out that even Sugar Blasted Crunchy Flakes didn't look good at breakfast. He **ate like a bird.**

"**Hold your horses!**" hollers Emma. "We can study together. If we quiz each other all night long, I bet we'll do great on that test."

"I won't **count my chickens before they're hatched,**" says Aiden. "But it's worth a try!"

Monkeys? Beavers? Cows? Chickens? What's up with that? Nothing you won't understand once you get clued into the world of idioms. <u>Idioms are phrases that mean something different from what you might think they mean.</u> Sometimes these phrases can seem super confusing. But when you learn what idioms mean (and where the heck they come from), they're not so confusing after all. So read on and learn all you can about idioms—**straight from the horse's mouth.**

AS SICK as a DOG

Ethan is as sick as a dog. He certainly doesn't look like a dog. Dogs are furry and walk on four legs. They stick out their tongues a lot.

Ethan doesn't look too great right now. But even though he sometimes sticks out his tongue (especially at his older sister), he is not a dog.

Sick as a dog just means **"extremely ill."** The expression started because dogs eat a lot of things they shouldn't—rotten food from the garbage; crumbs you drop on the floor; and even stuff that isn't food, like sock fuzz. These things often make dogs very sick. So to be sick as a dog means you're very sick indeed. And it often means that the place you feel most sick is your stomach.

If you're sick as a dog, you'll probably want to stay in bed!

CROCODILE TEARS

Jenna's bratty little brother, Jayden, wails and cries. He throws himself on the floor, demanding a cookie. The tears begin to puddle. "Don't worry," says Jenna's mom. "Those are nothing but crocodile tears."

Crocodile tears? Is Jenna's brother turning into a reptile? Well, he's always been a little strange. But this would be *really* strange. So why is Jenna's mom so calm? It's because she knows Jenna's brother isn't really that upset, even though he's freaking out. **Crocodile tears is an expression that means "fake tears."** He's just crying because he can't have a cookie. He thinks tears might help his chances. (Boy, does he have a lot to learn.)

But what do phony tears have to do with crocodiles? <u>It turns out that crocs are masters of crying fake tears.</u> Scientists believe these reptiles can make their eyes well up and drip fake tears into their mouths. No, they're not trying to convince their mothers to give them cookies. And they're not unhappy either. They use the tears to moisten their food and make it easier to chew and swallow.

Crocodiles like to feed on anything that moves. This can include other reptiles, birds, and even mammals as large as elephants. Crocs hold down their prey under water until it drowns. Then they start chomping. As a croc chews, tears help the food slide down its throat. But Jenna doesn't have to worry. Little brothers have never been known to use crocodile tears to help them swallow large mammals. Mostly, little brothers just want cookies.

Little kids (and sometimes even bigger kids!) might use crocodile tears to try to get their way.

WHITE ELEPHANT

Luis's dad is gift wrapping the ugliest lamp Luis has ever seen. In fact, Luis remembers when that lamp used to be in the basement near the sofa. But then his mom decided it was too ugly for even the basement.

A super-ugly lamp might be considered a white elephant.

"Uh, Dad?" Luis says. "Isn't it kind of mean to give someone that ugly lamp as a present?" But Luis's dad just laughs. "Don't worry," he says. "It's a white elephant gift. Your mom and I are going to a white elephant gift exchange at the neighbors'."

What does Luis's dad mean? The lamp clearly isn't an elephant. It isn't even white! And what kind of gift exchange would involve swapping elephants with the neighbors?

All his dad means is that the gift doesn't have any value. **A white elephant is something worthless.** A white elephant gift exchange is an event where people give one another worthless—and often funny—presents just for laughs.

Why do we call a worthless item a white elephant? This saying goes all the way back to ancient Burma. In this Southeast Asian country (officially called Myanmar in modern times), white elephants have long been considered sacred. They supposedly bring good luck to their owners. But since they're sacred, they can't be put to work, as elephants often are in Asia. Instead, an owner of a white elephant is expected to shower the animal with care and expensive ornaments. As a result, a white elephant became a gift to give your biggest enemy. It was a way of bankrupting an enemy, who would be forced to spend a fortune caring for the animal.

These days, we don't give white elephant gifts to enemies. Instead, we give them to friends and family at white-elephant-themed events. Some people even have white elephant gift exchanges at Christmas or on other holidays to have a little fun. The ugliest or the goofiest white elephant gifts are usually considered the best. That lamp of Luis's dad's should be a winner!

Real white elephants were a burden in ancient Burma because they were believed to need extra-special—and extra-expensive!—care.

HOLD Your HORSES

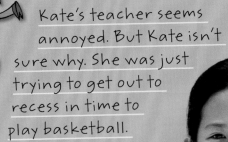

Kate's teacher seems annoyed. But Kate isn't sure why. She was just trying to get out to recess in time to play basketball.

Sure, she heard her teacher call, "Hold your horses, Kate!" But Kate just kept right on going. After all, she didn't have any horses to hold. Now Kate's teacher looks exasperated.

What did Kate's teacher mean when she told Kate to hold her horses? She meant that Kate should slow down. **Saying "hold your horses" is a pretty common way of telling people not to rush.** Whoops. No wonder Kate's teacher is giving her the evil eye.

Why do people say "hold your horses" when they mean to slow down? Some historians think it comes from a time when people really did have to hold their horses to slow themselves down.

People once traveled mostly by horse and buggy. To get their buggies to move more slowly, they'd hold tightly to the reins on their horses, which would keep the horses from galloping off.

Others think the expression comes from the military. In the days of cannons and cavalry (soldiers who fought on horseback), the cavalry would often line up behind the cannons. The cavalry soldiers had to make sure they held on to their horses when the cannons fired. Otherwise, the noise would spook the horses and make them rush forward.

Back in the day, people held on to their horses' reins when they wanted to move slowly.

MONKEY on Your BACK

Aashi is super confused. She's been in a fight with her best friend for nearly a week. She asked her grandmother for advice. But instead of helping her solve the problem, her grandma called Aashi's friend a monkey!

Actually, Aashi's grandma said: "This fight with your friend is a monkey on your back. You need to talk to her and set things right." But why did her grandma change the subject like that? And does she *really* think her friend is a monkey?

Aashi's grandma isn't calling anybody a monkey. She's using the expression *monkey on your back* to mean a problem that won't go away. People often use this phrase to describe an ongoing issue that they're worried about.

What does a monkey have to do with an ongoing problem? Well, let's think about it. <u>If you had a monkey on your back, it would be really hard to get it off, right?</u> Monkeys have those long arms. They could wrap their arms around your neck. You might try to shake them off, but they'd cling on. Maybe you'd try to reach back and grab the monkey. Still, he'd probably be able to hang on. You'd have to take really drastic action to get a monkey off your back. That's why people use the phrase "monkey on your back" to refer to problems that won't go away.

The more Aashi thinks about it, the more she can see how her fight with her friend really is like a monkey on her back. It isn't going to go away unless she takes charge and does something. She thinks she'll call her friend today. After all, it'll be hard to sleep tonight if she has a monkey on her back!

Monkeys have superlong arms. If a monkey really was on your back, it could cling to you pretty tightly.

As BUSY as a BEAVER

"You look as busy as a beaver," Joe's teacher tells him. But Joe looks nothing like a beaver. He doesn't have a bushy tail. He doesn't have hair all over his body. What the heck does his teacher mean? And is being busy as a beaver good or bad?

Busy as a beaver just means "really, really busy." Joe's teacher noticed that Joe's busy trying to finish his reading worksheet. In this case, being busy as a beaver is definitely good!

This kid's as busy as a beaver. That means he's very busy!

It's a sign that Joe's teacher thinks he's doing what he's supposed to be doing (unlike that time last week when Joe got caught playing Creature of the Swamp with his buddy during class).

So why do people say "busy as a beaver" when they just mean "busy"? It's because beavers are known to be one of Earth's busiest animals. They're always working on building their dams. They use gnawed branches and mud from the bottoms of streams. If they find any broken shells or other objects, they add those in too. Since water constantly washes away at their dams, their work is never done.

A beaver is always building. Its work is never done!

Until the COWS Come HOME

Oh boy. Chen's mom's upset again. She can't stand it when Chen's sister refuses to eat her dinner!

Every night it's the same old thing. Chen's sister sits stubbornly in her chair, and their mom just gets madder and madder. "You'd better eat those peas!" she practically hollers. "I'll wait until the cows come home if I have to."

Now Chen sits up. Cows coming home? **Last time he checked, there were no cows living anywhere near his apartment building.** What could his mother possibly mean?

This kid hates peas! Waiting for her to eat them is like waiting till the cows come home.

Chen's mom isn't expecting any cows to come to their front door. She's just using an expression she might've heard when she was a kid. **People say "until the cows come home" when they mean a really, really long time.**

The expression "until the cows come home" became popular when a lot of people lived on farms and kept cows for milk. Each morning, they would milk the cows. Then they would let the cows wander off to eat grass and do whatever else cows do all day. Late in the evening, the cows would make their way back to the barn to be milked again. Milking the cows would often be the last chore of the day. And to many farmers, it seemed as if they had to wait forever for the cows to return for the evening milking. So farmers started using the expression "until the cows come home" to mean "an extremely long time."

When cows start eating grass, there's no telling when they might come back to the barn!

CRY WOLF

Carlos's mom slammed the car door, and his little brother, Oscar, pretended she'd crushed his fingers. "Ow, ow!" Oscar cried, holding his hand. "I think it's broken."

Carlos and Oscar's mom looked alarmed—really, really scared, in fact. So Oscar laughed to show her it was just a joke. But their mom didn't see the humor. In fact, she was pretty angry.

"Oscar, if you keep crying wolf like that, I'm never going to believe you when you really are hurt!" she exclaimed. Then *Oscar* looked offended. "Don't insult my acting skills," he said. "I wasn't even trying to act like a wolf!" Boy, was that the wrong thing to say. Carlos and Oscar's mom looked really mad then.

Sly wolves, like this one, have been known to nab a sheep or two for dinner.

Of course, their mom didn't really think Oscar was acting like a wolf. Instead, she was accusing him of falsely calling for help. That's what people mean when they say "crying wolf."

Crying wolf comes from an old fable by Aesop called "The Boy Who Cried Wolf." In the story, a shepherd boy gets bored as he's watching his flock of sheep. One day, for excitement, he calls for help. He yells that a wolf is attacking his flock. When his neighbors come running to his aid, they are mad that he

Don't yell for help for no reason. You never know when you really will need someone's help someday!

falsely called for help. But he doesn't learn his lesson. He cries wolf a few more times, and each time his neighbors get angry. Then a wolf really does attack his flock. He yells and yells for help. But of course, nobody comes. They had grown tired of him crying wolf.

Straight from the HORSE'S MOUTH

"Ms. Johnson! " Ana cried. "Sam just called me a horse."

"Sam!" called Ms. Johnson. "Come to my desk. I'm sending you to the principal's office."

The principal's office? Again? How unfair! This time, Sam really didn't do anything. It was all just a big mix-up.

Ana had told Sam all about the new movie she'd seen. Then Sam told his friends he'd heard about the movie straight from the horse's mouth. He didn't mean Ana was a horse. **All he meant was that he got his information from a good source.** That's what it means to say you heard something straight from the horse's mouth.

This horse's mouth might look kind of icky. But saying you heard something from the horse's mouth means you have a good source!

So how did "straight from the horse's mouth" come to mean "you got your info from someone who has all the facts"? <u>Well, the expression comes from horse traders. They can tell how old a horse is by looking at the horse's teeth.</u> Before they pay a lot of money for a horse, they want to be sure they know how old it is. Since the seller might lie, a buyer will look right into the horse's mouth to examine its teeth. Then the trader has the information straight from the horse's mouth.

Horse traders often check out a horse's molars before paying good money for the animal. A horse's teeth give a good idea of how old the horse is.

Don't Let the CAT Out of the BAG

"Don't let the cat out of the bag," Hakeem's mother calls to him as she leaves for the store.

Hakeem's mom is going to get food for a surprise party for his dad. Meanwhile, Hakeem is supposed to blow up party balloons in his room so his dad doesn't see them. Then, when his mom gets back home, he's supposed to ask his dad to take a walk with him so his mom can set up the party. But now his mom also wants him to worry about a cat in a bag? *What's up with that?* Hakeem wonders. **We don't even have a cat!**

But all Hakeem's mother meant was that Hakeem shouldn't spoil the surprise.

Uh-oh, this cat's already partly out of the bag!

Sellers at marketplaces in the Middle Ages sometimes passed off cheap cats as expensive pigs. They kept the cats in bags so the buyers didn't know what they were buying.

Don't let the cat out of the bag is just another way of saying "Don't let the secret out."

This expression began way back in the Middle Ages, more than a thousand years ago. Sellers at marketplaces used cats wrapped up in fabric bags to try to trick buyers. The buyers thought they were buying a pig. The sellers would take their money and give them a bag with an animal squirming around inside. The sellers would tell them not to open the bag until they got home. But once they got home, the buyers would discover that they had paid a lot of money for a cat instead of a pig. If they had "let the cat out of the bag" earlier, they would have discovered the secret.

GET Your GOAT

Bree's annoying younger cousin is at it again. He won't stop teasing her about her new glasses. Bree tries to ignore him, but finally she can't take it anymore.

"Stop it, you idiot!" she yells at him.

"Oh, Bree," their grandpa says. "Don't let your cousin get your goat."

Has Bree's whole family gone crazy? Why is her grandpa talking about goats? Well, actually, he isn't—not really, anyway. **Get your goat is just an expression that means "to annoy."** Bree's grandpa is advising her to not let her cousin annoy her.

Goats are calm creatures.
They help horses keep their cool.

So what does getting a goat have to do with being annoyed? Plenty, it turns out. Goats are mild-mannered animals. They are often used to calm down other animals. Racehorse owners often put a goat in their horse's stall the night before a big race. The goat helps keep the horses calm. But some tricky competitors learned that if they steal their opponents' goats, their horses won't get a calming night's sleep. Instead, the horses are jittery and unable to race well the next day. So if you "get the goat" of another person, you make him too bothered to perform well.

EAT
Like a Bird

Alex hates it when his aunt tells him he eats like a bird. Sure, Alex knows he doesn't chow down on five slices of pizza at a time as his older brothers do. But there's no need to call him a bird.

Kids who don't eat a whole lot in one sitting might hear the expression, "You eat like a bird."

Birds just peck at their food with their beaks. Alex uses a knife and a fork. Besides, Alex is pretty sure that birds eat seeds and nuts and things like that. Alex does enjoy some sunflower seeds every now and then, but he eats a lot more than just seeds!

But Alex's aunt isn't commenting on whether Alex uses silverware—or even on what foods he eats. She's just teasing him a little because he doesn't eat very much.

The expression eat *like a bird* means "to eat just a small amount."

The saying got started because most people agree that birds eat very little. Birds are pretty small, and if you've ever watched them at a bird feeder, you know that they often eat just a few bites and then fly away. But in fact, birds eat quite a lot—especially for their size.

Consider this: Most birds weigh just over a pound (454 grams). And they often eat about a pound of food each day. By comparison, the average human weighs about 140 pounds (64 kilograms). But a human would never eat 140 pounds of food a day. In fact, eating that much food in a day would be very, very bad for you!

The next time Alex's aunt tells him he eats like a bird, maybe he should let her know that his dining habits are nothing like those of the birds at her backyard feeder. In fact, Alex's brothers eat a lot more like birds than he does!

Contrary to popular belief, birds eat a lot.

Don't Count Your CHICKENS Before They're HATCHED

Pilar's class has sold the most items so far in their school's bake sale. Everybody's getting excited because the class that sells the most wins an ice-cream party! Pilar and her friends start talking about their favorite ice-cream flavors.

"Wait a minute now," their teacher, Mr. Nguyen, tells them. "Don't start counting your chickens before they're hatched. The bake sale still has another hour to go."

Why is Mr. Nguyen talking about chickens? The class is selling cupcakes, brownies, and cookies. What do chickens have to do with anything? Not much—and Mr. Nguyen knows that!

This cutie has hatched and is ready to be counted.

Smart farmers never count on all their eggs hatching.

He's just telling the class not to count on things before they are certain. That's all "don't count your chickens before they're hatched" means.

This popular saying got its start from farmers who raised chickens. Once their hens laid eggs, the farmers knew that they couldn't count on every egg hatching. <u>They had to wait to see how many chickens would actually hatch out of the eggs.</u> Farmers who got too excited and started counting the eggs were "counting their chickens before they hatched."

Glossary

cavalry: soldiers who fought on horseback

dam: a strong barrier built across a stream or a river to hold back water. Beavers build dams.

flock: a group of animals of one kind that live, travel, or feed together

idiom: a commonly used expression or phrase that means something different from what it appears to mean

mammal: a warm-blooded animal with a backbone. Female mammals produce milk to feed their young.

prey: an animal that another animal hunts for food

reptile: a cold-blooded animal that crawls across the ground or creeps on short legs. Reptiles have backbones and reproduce by laying eggs.

sacred: holy or very important

shepherd: someone whose job is to look after sheep

source: someone or something that provides information

Further Reading

Cleary, Brian P. *Skin Like Milk, Hair of Silk: What Are Similes and Metaphors?*
Minneapolis: Millbrook Press, 2009. This cute picture book explains similies and
metaphors—figures of speech that can sometimes seem confusing!

Doeden, Matt. *Put on Your Thinking Cap: And Other Expressions about School.*
Minneapolis: Lerner Publications Company, 2013. Come along as Doeden explores
the story behind thirteen fun expressions related to school.

Heos, Bridget. *Cool as a Cucumber: And Other Expressions about Food.*
Minneapolis: Lerner Publications Company, 2013. Heos introduces food-related
expressions and gives interesting explanations of where they came from.

Idioms and Their Meanings
http://www.buzzle.com/articles/idioms-and-their-meanings.html
Uncover new idioms in this list of the meanings and roots of idioms used in the
United States.

Idioms by Kids
http://www.idiomsbykids.com
Check out more than one thousand kid-drawn pictures of the literal meanings of
idioms. You can add your own examples too.

Idiom Site
http://www.idiomsite.com
Search this alphabetical list of idioms and their meanings.

Moses, Will. *Raining Cats and Dogs.* New York: Philomel Books, 2008. Entertaining
text and whimsical art help explain some common but puzzling sayings.

Paint by Idioms
http://www.funbrain.com/funbrain/idioms
Test your knowledge of common idioms by taking the multiple-choice quizzes on
this site from FunBrain.

Terban, Marvin. *In a Pickle: And Other Funny Idioms.* New York: Clarion Books, 2007.
This book uncovers the real meaning behind a number of everyday expressions.

Terban, Marvin. *Scholastic Dictionary of Idioms* (Rev. ed.). New York: Scholastic,
2006. Look up explanations for more than seven hundred idioms in this reference
book with alphabetical listings and an index.

Index

Photo Acknowledgments

The images in this book are used with the permission of: © plainpicture/Siegfried Kuttig, p. 5; © Anup Shah/Digital Vision/Getty Images, p. 6; © iStockphoto.com/selimaksan, p. 7; © iStockphoto.com/RonTech2000, p. 8; AP Photo/Khin Maung Win, p. 9; © Stockbyte/Getty Images, pp. 10–11; © Lisa F. Young/Alamy, p. 11 (top); © Bettmann/CORBIS, p. 11 (bottom); © Brad Wilson/Iconica/Getty Images, p. 13; © Comstock Images/Getty Images, p. 14; © Wildlife/Alamy, p. 15; © D. Anschutz/Digital Vision/Getty Images, p. 16; © Laurent Renault/Dreamstime.com, p. 17; © Richard Rondeau/Dreamstime.com, p. 18; © iStockphoto.com/Sava Alexandru, p. 19 (top); © Brendan Ó Sé/Flickr/Getty Images, p. 19 (bottom); © Studio 37/Dreamstime.com, p. 20; © Maeers/Hulton Archive/Getty Images, p. 21; © Mark Ross/Alamy, p. 22; © Silvio Fiore/SuperStock, p. 23; © Juniors Bildarchiv/Alamy, p. 25 (top); © Bonnie Sue Rauch/Photo Researchers, p. 25 (bottom); © Radius Images/Alamy, p. 26; © John Van Decker/Alamy, p. 27; © iStockphoto.com/Plainview, p. 28; © Keystone View Company/FPG/Archive Photos/Getty Images, p. 29.

Front cover: © iStockphoto.com/Bob Ainsworth (left); © Lauren Burke/Photographer's Choice RF/Getty Images (center); © Pam Francis/Photographer's Choice/Getty Images (right).

Main body text set in Adrianna Light 11/17.
Typeface provided by Chank.

How
Does Energy
Work?

Investigating
Electricity

Sally M. Walker

Lerner Publications Company
Minneapolis

Author's note: The experiments in this book use the metric measurement system, as that's the system most commonly used by scientists.

Lerner Publications Company
A division of Lerner Publishing Group, Inc.
241 First Avenue North
Minneapolis, MN 55401 U.S.A.

Website address: www.lernerbooks.com

Library of Congress Cataloging-in-Publication Data

Walker, Sally M.
      Investigating Electricity / by Sally M. Walker.
          p.   cm. — (Searchlight books™—how does energy work?)
      Includes index.
      ISBN 978–0–7613–5772–8 (lib. bdg. : alk. paper)
      1. Electricity—Juvenile literature. I. Title.
   QC527.2 .W356 2012
   537—dc22   2010035819

Manufactured in the United States of America
1 – DP – 7/15/11

Contents

Chapter 1

PEOPLE AND ELECTRICITY

Long ago, people lit their homes with candles. Now we use electricity. Electricity is a form of energy. It can be used in many ways.

How do people use electricity?

Look around you. What electrical things can you see?
Lights? A computer? A TV?

Electricity powers lamps,
computers, and many other
things around a home.

Safety First

Electricity is helpful. But it can be dangerous! So remember these safety rules. Don't touch electrical outlets. Keep electrical wires away from water. Don't touch cracked wires. Go inside during a thunderstorm. Lightning is electricity.

Electricity is powerful. It can hurt or even kill people.

The experiments in this book are safe. But before doing them, talk with an adult. He or she might like to help you experiment.

ALL SCIENTISTS NEED TO STAY SAFE. IT'S SMART TO HAVE AN ADULT'S HELP WHEN YOU DO EXPERIMENTS.

Chapter 2

AMAZING ATOMS

When you turn on a lamp, electricity lights the bulb. But where does electricity begin? It begins inside atoms. Atoms are tiny particles. They are so small you can't see them.

How does electricity make a lamp light up?

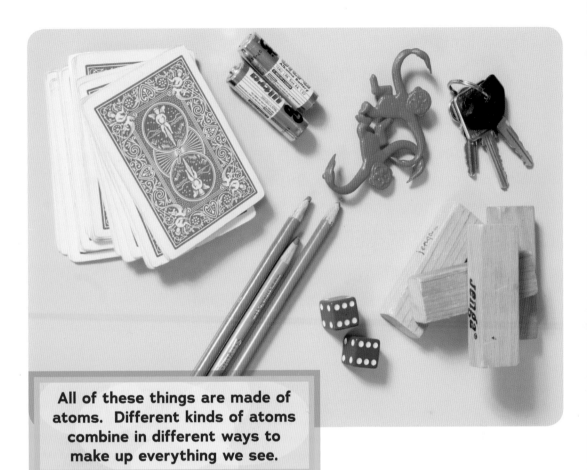

All of these things are made of atoms. Different kinds of atoms combine in different ways to make up everything we see.

Everything around you is made of atoms. There are different kinds of atoms. And they can join together in different ways. That's why we have different substances, like air, apples, and toys.

9

Three Parts

An atom has three parts. The parts are protons, electrons, and neutrons. Protons and electrons have electrical energy. A proton's energy is called a positive charge. An electron's energy is called a negative charge. Neutrons have no charge. The whole atom doesn't have a charge either. That's because the protons and the electrons balance each other out.

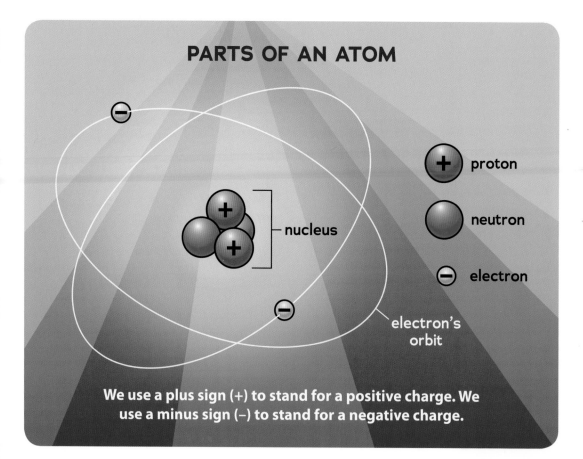

PARTS OF AN ATOM

nucleus

proton

neutron

electron

electron's orbit

We use a plus sign (+) to stand for a positive charge. We use a minus sign (–) to stand for a negative charge.

These boys and girls are standing near one another. They are like protons and neutrons crowded together in an atom's nucleus. If they are the nucleus, where would the electrons be in this picture?

Protons and neutrons are in an atom's center. This center is called the nucleus. Electrons circle around the nucleus. Their path is called an orbit. Some electrons circle close to the nucleus. Others circle farther away.

Free Electrons

Rubbing objects together can move electrons.
Sometimes an electron gets knocked out of its orbit.
Then it is called a free electron.

When you pet a dog, you may be moving electrons around. Rubbing the animal's fur can bump the electrons.

A free electron may jump to another atom. Atoms that gain or lose electrons become ions. An ion is an atom with an electrical charge. Ions with extra electrons have a negative charge. Ions with too few electrons have a positive charge.

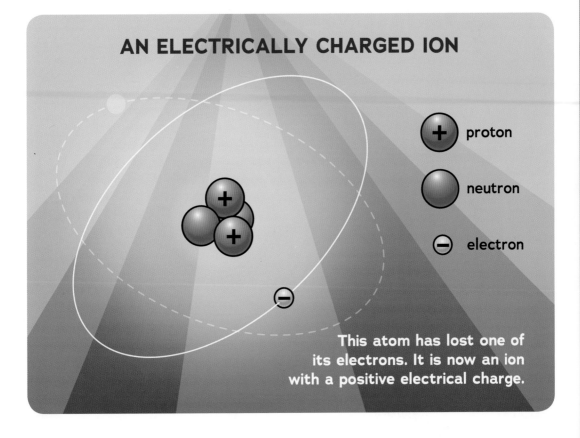

AN ELECTRICALLY CHARGED ION

proton

neutron

electron

This atom has lost one of its electrons. It is now an ion with a positive electrical charge.

Chapter 3

ELECTRIC CHARGE

Most objects have no charge. But an object can become charged when it loses or gains electrons. See for yourself.

Experiment Time!

You'll need two balloons, a sheet of paper, a 41-centimeter-long piece of string, a yardstick, a marker, and a scissors.

How can you use these simple things to make an electrical charge?

Draw several penny-sized circles on the paper. Cut the circles out. Put them on a table. Draw an *X* on each balloon. Blow up both balloons. Tie them shut.

Pick up one of the balloons. Rub the *X* against your hair fifteen times. Rubbing makes some electrons in your hair leave their orbits. These free electrons move from your hair to the balloon. The spot marked with an *X* on the balloon has extra electrons. It has a negative charge.

There are millions of electrons in every strand of your hair. Rubbing the balloon against your hair bumps those electrons.

Hold the balloon's *X* about 2.5 centimeters above the paper circles. What happens? The circles jump to the balloon. Why?

Watch the paper circles closely.

Static electricity makes the paper stick to the balloon.

Static Electricity

Static electricity holds the circles to the balloon. Static electricity is energy created between objects with different, or unlike, charges. Unlike charges pull toward each other.

The part of the balloon you marked with an *X* has a negative charge. That negative charge pulls positive charges in the circles toward the balloon. Static electricity forms. It holds the circles and the balloon together.

Two objects with the same kind of charge have like charges. Like charges push away from each other.

Prove It

Tie one end of the string around the knot of one balloon. Tie the other end around one end of the yardstick. Put the yardstick on a table so the balloon hangs down. Lift the balloon. Rub the marked *X* on your hair fifteen times. Let go of the balloon.

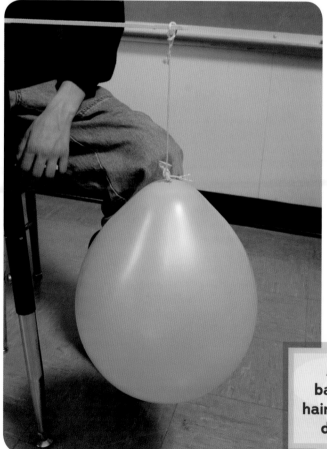

After rubbing the balloon against your hair, let it hang straight down on its string.

Pick up the other balloon. Rub its X on your hair fifteen times. Try to touch the X on this balloon to the X on the hanging balloon. (Don't touch the hanging balloon with your hand.) What happens? The X on the hanging balloon moves away from the balloon in your hand. Why? Both balloons have a negative charge. Like charges push away from each other.

You can use static electricity to move the hanging balloon without even touching it.

Chapter 4

CURRENTS AND CIRCUITS

Static electricity lasts only a short time. It needs more free electrons to last. When you stopped rubbing the balloon on your hair, free electrons stopped moving to the balloon. That meant the static electricity stopped too. But if electrons keep moving to the balloon, electricity can last. A steady flow of free electrons is called a current.

Static electricity can make your hair stand up like this, but only for a little while. Why doesn't static electricity last very long?

Current moves when free electrons from one atom pass to the next. Let's see how this works. Stand in a row with your friends. Whisper a word to the person next to you. If everyone whispers the word to the next person, the word reaches the end of the line. Current flows along a wire the same way. The wire's atoms stay in place as the free electrons flow from one atom to the next.

No one moves out of place in your line. But the word you whisper moves from person to person. This is how electricity moves too.

Conductors

Current flows easily through some materials. These materials are called conductors. Silver and copper are conductors.

This copper wire is a good conductor. It carries electric current well.

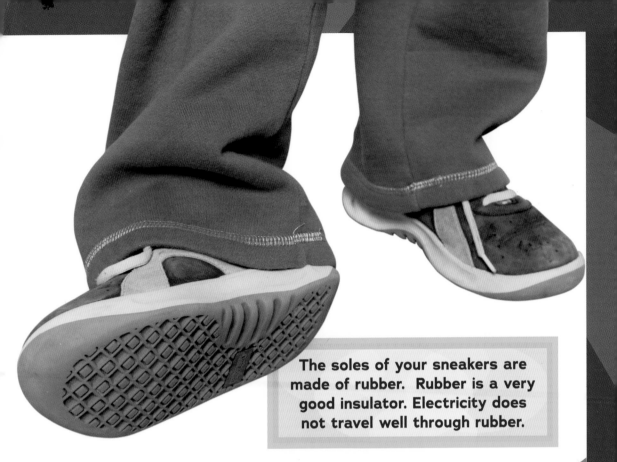

The soles of your sneakers are made of rubber. Rubber is a very good insulator. Electricity does not travel well through rubber.

Insulators

Some materials don't carry current well. These materials are called insulators. Wood and rubber are insulators. An insulator can protect you from getting a shock. Rubber is wrapped around wires to keep their current from hurting people.

What Makes a Current?

You made static electricity when you rubbed a balloon against your hair. But where does a current come from?

Putting certain materials together can make a current. These materials are inside batteries. They make electricity inside the battery.

Batteries come in all shapes and sizes. What have you used batteries for? A flashlight? A video game?

You can use a battery to make a current flow. You'll need a size D battery, a flashlight bulb, a clothespin, clear tape, and a sheet of aluminum foil.

HOW CAN THESE THINGS MAKE ELECTRICITY FLOW? FIND OUT!

Trying It Out

Fold the foil into a strip. Look at the battery. The bumpy end of the battery is called the positive terminal. The flat end is the negative terminal. Feel each terminal. Are they warm? No. But you can make them get warm by making a current.

Right now, the battery feels cool to the touch. But flowing electricity makes heat.

Tape one end of the foil strip across the negative terminal. Did the terminal feel warm? No. Hold the other end of the foil across the positive terminal. Are the terminals getting warm? Yes. That's because current is flowing. Currents make heat.

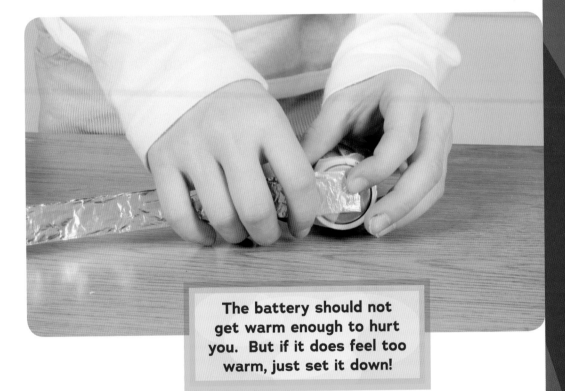

The battery should not get warm enough to hurt you. But if it does feel too warm, just set it down!

The loop of foil connects the two terminals. It makes a path from one end of the battery to the other.

The current flowed because you made a path for it to follow. This path is called a circuit. Electricity needs a circuit to flow. The circuit must connect the battery's positive and negative terminals. The circuit must also be closed. A closed circuit is a path without spaces in it.

Closed and Open Circuits

Use one hand to make a circle with your thumb and index finger. Can you trace all the way around the circle with the index finger of your other hand? Yes! Your fingers make a closed circuit.

Holding your fingers in an OK sign can help you think about what a closed circuit looks like. Your fingers make a complete loop.

Spread your thumb and index finger apart. This time, there's a space between your fingers. You can't trace a complete circle. Your fingers don't make a closed circuit.

Hold your fingers apart. They do not make a complete loop. There is a gap, or space. There is also a gap in circuits that are not closed.

Closing a Circuit

Look at your battery and the foil strip. One end of the strip is taped to the negative terminal. The other end is not touching the positive terminal. You can't trace along the foil from one terminal to the other without lifting your finger. It isn't a closed circuit. How could you close the circuit?

The foil is not making a complete circuit. The loop does not go all the way from the negative terminal to the positive terminal. Electricity cannot travel through the strip.

Hold the loose end of the foil against the positive terminal. Can you trace along the foil from one terminal to the other without lifting your finger? Yes. You have made a closed circuit. You know this because the terminals are warm. That means current is flowing. Current flows only through a closed circuit.

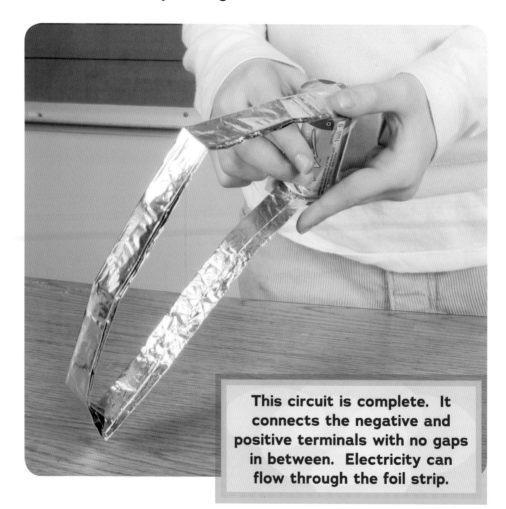

This circuit is complete. It connects the negative and positive terminals with no gaps in between. Electricity can flow through the foil strip.

Currents on the Move

To flow, a current needs a closed circuit. But what makes the current move? Free electrons need a push to get moving. That push comes from electrical force. Electrical force is measured in volts. Your battery has 1.5 volts. That's enough force to push electrical charges along the foil.

Look for the word *volts* or the letter *V* on your battery. Every battery has a certain number of volts. The more volts a battery has, the more of a "push" it can give to an electric current.

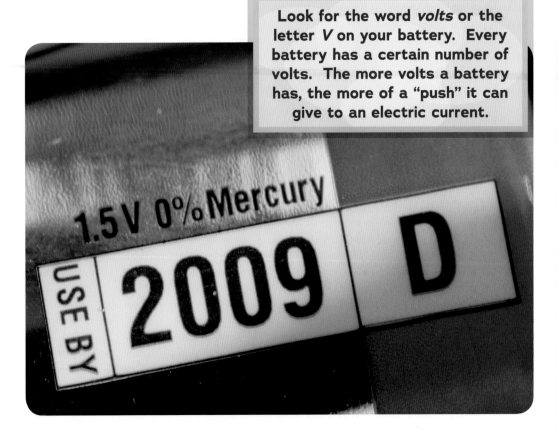

Volts force current to keep flowing. Flowing current will light your flashlight bulb. But to do this, you need a closed circuit.

Experiment Time Again!

Wrap the loose end of the foil around the metal part of the bulb. Clamp the foil in place with the clothespin. Make sure the other end of the foil is taped to the negative terminal.

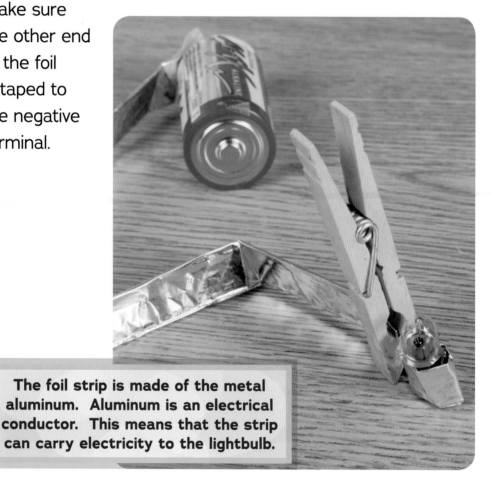

The foil strip is made of the metal aluminum. Aluminum is an electrical conductor. This means that the strip can carry electricity to the lightbulb.

Does the bulb light if you touch the contact to the side of the battery? No, because the battery is covered in plastic. Plastic is an insulator.

The metal point on the bottom of the bulb is called the contact. The metal contact is a good conductor.

Touch the bulb's contact to the negative terminal on the battery. The terminal's metal also is a good conductor. Does the bulb light? No. It doesn't light because the negative terminal is not connected to the positive terminal. You haven't made a closed circuit yet.

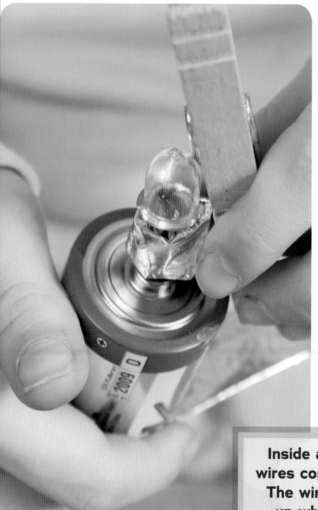

Touch the contact to the positive terminal. Does the bulb light? Yes! The circuit is closed. Current flows from the negative terminal. It flows through the foil to the bulb and then on to the positive terminal. The circuit is complete. Current flows through the wires inside the bulb and makes it light up.

Inside a lightbulb are two straight wires connected by a thin, curly wire. The wire glows and the bulb lights up when the circuit is complete.

Electricity is useful for running machines and making heat. It can also make light. And that's useful for reading a book at night!

Next time you read by a lamp, think about how electricity works!

Glossary

atom: a very tiny particle that makes up all things

charge: the energy of an atom or part of an atom. When atoms gain or lose electrons, they gain a charge.

circuit: the path that an electric current follows

conductor: a material that carries electric current well

current: the flow of electricity through something

electron: the part of an atom that has a negative charge. Electrons circle around the center of the atom.

insulator: a material that does not carry electric current well

ion: an atom that has gained or lost electrons

negative charge: the charge that a substance has if its atoms have gained extra electrons from other atoms

nucleus: the center of an atom. The nucleus is made of protons and neutrons.

orbit: a circular or oval path. Electrons follow an orbit around the center of an atom.

particle: a tiny piece

positive charge: the charge that a substance has if its atoms have lost electrons to other atoms

static electricity: energy created between objects that have different electric charges

terminal: one of the ends of a battery. Every battery has a positive terminal and a negative terminal.

Learn More about Electricity

Books

Jango-Cohen, Judith. *Ben Franklin's Big Shock*. Minneapolis: Millbrook Press, 2006. Learn all about Ben Franklin's interest in and experiments with electricity.

Moore, Rob. *Why Does Electricity Flow?: All about Electricity*. New York: PowerKids Press, 2010. This engaging book explores science mysteries related to electricity.

Spilsbury, Richard. *What Is Electricity and Magnetism?: Exploring Science with Hands-On Activities*. Berkeley Heights, NJ: Enslow Elementary, 2008. Check out this title to find more electricity experiments you can try.

Waring, Geoff. *Oscar and the Bird: A Book about Electricity*. Cambridge, MA: Candlewick Press, 2009. Waring takes a playful look at electricity.

Websites

Enchanted Learning: Static Electricity
http://www.enchantedlearning.com/physics/Staticelectricity.shtml
Read up on static electricity at this page from Enchanted Learning.

Energy Kids: History of Energy
http://www.eia.doe.gov/kids/energy.cfm?page=4
This website from the Energy Information Administration has timelines exploring important discoveries about energy.

The NASA SciFiles: Electricity Activities
http://scifiles.larc.nasa.gov/text/kids/D_Lab/acts_electric.html
This NASA site features several fun activities for learning about electricity.

Index

Photo Acknowledgments

Photographs copyright © Andy King. Additional images in this book are used with the permission of: © Jack Hollingsworth/Getty Images, p. 5; © Wolfe Larry/Shutterstock Images, p. 6; © Laura Westlund/Independent Picture Service, pp. 10, 13.

Front Cover: © Todd Strand/Independent Picture Service.

Main body text set in Adrianna Regular 14/20.
Typeface provided by Chank.